Innsky Air Fryer Oven Cookbook

Crispy, Easy, and Delicious Innsky Air Fryer Oven Recipes for Smart People

Banden Mancine

Table of Contents

Introduction

Fried food is delicious, and most people will definitely agree.

Unfortunately, it is also one of the unhealthiest foods you can ever eat. One way to mimic the taste of fried food is by air frying.

An air fryer is basically a small convection oven. Unlike ovens, air fryers are compact and will not heat up your entire kitchen every time you use it. Air fryers use significantly less oil in cooking and may even reduce the amount of oil in your food.

Air fryers are excellent for people with limited space since they are multifunction appliances and only take up a fraction of the counter space. They are highly versatile, letting you cook a wide range of dishes.

In fact, most people who bought air fryers have found themselves cooking with it more frequently than their other appliances because it is easy to operate, yields terrific flavors, and is a breeze to clean.

With an air fryer, you'll be able to cook delectable meals quickly, reheat leftovers, and feel better because you know you're making healthier meals for your family.

Chapter 1: Overview of Innsky Air Fryer Oven

What is Innsky Air Fryer Oven?

The Innsky air fryer oven is a multi-cooker that can bake, fry, roast, and grill. It also functions as an oven since it rapidly cooks with hot circulating air. It has seven presets for steak, chicken, shrimp, seafood, vegetables, bread, and French fries. It also has an option for frozen food, delay start, preheat, and keep warm.

One of the first things you'll notice is the exterior, which is made of elegant and durable stainless steel. The touch LED screen is responsive, stylish, and modern looking. Apart from the one-touch presets, it also has buttons to adjust the time and temperature. The temperature ranges from 180 to 400 degrees Fahrenheit, letting you cook a wide array of foods in less time.

Air fryers are healthier options than regular deep fryers since it uses little to no oil. It can cook foods up to four times faster, retaining more nutrients than other conventional cooking methods. Innsky's air fryers are made with good quality materials that are durable and will last.

The frying basket and pan have a non-stick coating that is BPA-free and dishwasher-safe. The inner housing is also made from food-grade stainless steel. It has a large capacity of 5.8 quarts, an ideal size for a family of five. The frying basket can fit a 6-lbs whole chicken for roasting. The square shape of the fryer basket is able to accommodate more ingredients compared to round-shaped air fryers.

How to Use the Innsky Air Fryer Oven

Follow these steps when you are about to use your air fryer for the first time.

1. After removing all packaging, plastics, and stickers, gently remove the frying pan

and basket and wash them thoroughly in hot soapy water.

2. Use only non-abrasive sponges for cleaning to avoid scratching or damaging the nonstick coating.

3. Use a clean damp cloth to wipe the exterior and interior of the air fryer.

4. Place the air fryer on a level and stable countertop that can withstand heat. Make sure that there are at least 4 inches of space around the appliance, especially at the back, to let heat escape while in use.

Cooking with your air fryer:

- Plug the air fryer onto an electrical outlet. Then tap the power button to turn it on.
- Tap the pre-heat button.
- Once pre-heating is done, remove the basket and place your ingredients inside. Make sure that the basket is properly installed with the pan.
- Place the basket back in the air fryer and choose a cooking mode suitable to your recipe.
- To begin the cooking cycle, press the start button.
- The timer will automatically pause when you take out the basket at any time within the cooking cycle and will resume when you put it back.
- The air fryer will beep once the cycle is done.
- Setting the time:
- You can customize the time to your preference by simply tapping the time option once and adjusting via the up and down arrows beside it. The time is set in 1-minute increments.
- You can tap start once you are ready to cook.
- Setting the temperature:
- Similar to how you set the time, adjust the temperature via the up and down arrows beside the temperature option. The temperature is set in 10-degree Fahrenheit

increments.

- Tap start once you are ready to cook.

Important reminders:

- You might notice a plastic smell with the first few uses. Do not worry as this is perfectly normal and will go away after a while.
- Pre-heating is best for most recipes but is not required every time you cook. Some foods like small cuts of vegetables, soft foods that you don't want to turn crunchy, or frozen meats can do away without pre-heating.
- If you forget to pre-heat when the recipe requires to do so, simply add a few minutes to your timer.
- Never overload the frying basket to get even cooking all throughout.
- Do not place a parchment paper inside the fryer while pre-heating. Only do this when you are ready to cook and with the ingredients laying on top of the parchment paper to prevent it from touching the heating element and cause flare-ups.

Safety Guidelines

Below are the manufacturer's guidelines to ensure the safe use of their product. Make sure to follow these tips at all times so you won't encounter any problems in the future.

- Place your air fryer in a level and stable surface away from any combustible materials. Leave ample space (at least 4 inches) around the appliance since it may become hot while in use.
- Before plugging in your Innsky air fryer oven, check if the voltage requirement of the appliance matches that of your electrical outlet.
- Check if all components, especially the cords, are free from damage. Do not plug in the appliance if you see any signs of damage.

- Make sure that the appliance is plugged in correctly and is away from hot surfaces and wet areas.

- Keep electrical components away from water and all other liquids. For safety, please avoid plugging in and operating the appliance with wet hands.

- The air fryer will beep once it is done cooking. Since the fryer is hot and steam may come out, use oven mitts and keep your head at a safe distance from the fryer when you are about to take out the food.

- Do not leave the electrical cord hanging or in an awkward position where it may cause people to trip.

- The appliance should not be operated by children unless they are supervised by an adult. Likewise, the appliance should only be operated by capable adults and should not be left unattended during use.

- The appliance should only be used indoors and in accordance to the manufacturer's guidelines. The use of any other device, accessory, or attachment, apart from the manufacturer's recommendation, may cause damage or harm.

- The air fryer should be unplugged when it is not in use and during cleaning. The appliance should be completely cooled down and unplugged from the outlet before you attempt to take out parts for cleaning and maintenance.

- If you encounter any malfunction, quickly unplug the appliance and contact customer support.

Care and Maintenance

Cleaning and maintaining the Innsky air fryer oven is fairly simple. Just remember to clean your air fryer every time you finish cooking to avoid any stubborn buildup of grease and debris. Follow these easy steps on how to clean and maintain your air fryer so it can last for a long time.

1. Unplug your air fryer from the electrical outlet and let it completely cool down.

2. Once cool, remove the frying basket and pan from the base.

3. Push the clear plastic cover forward to unlock, then push down the frying basket release button and lift the basket from the pan.

4. Soak the frying basket in hot soapy water for at least 10 minutes before washing to remove any leftovers. You may also put the hot soapy water on the frying pan itself then place the basket back to soak both parts at the same time.

5. Always use non-abrasive cleaners to preserve the nonstick coating.

6. Wash and rinse with cold water and thoroughly dry. You may also place these components in the dishwasher.

7. With a plastic brush, gently clean the heating element and the interior to remove any debris.

8. Wipe the interior and exterior with a clean damp cloth.

9. You may use a degreasing liquid for any dirt that is difficult to remove even after washing.

10. Store only when the appliance is thoroughly cleaned, and the parts have completely dried.

Chapter 2: Breakfast Recipes

Breakfast Frittata

Preparation Time: 15 minutes

Cooking Time: 20 minutes

Servings: 2

Ingredients:

- 4 eggs, beaten
- ¼ lb. breakfast sausage, cooked and crumbled
- 1 green onion, minced
- 2 tablespoons red bell pepper, diced
- ½ cup Monterey Jack cheese, shredded
- Cooking spray

Method:

1. In a bowl, mix all the ingredients.
2. Preheat your Innsky air fryer oven to 360 degrees F.
3. Spray a small cake pan with oil.
4. Pour the mixture into the cake pan.
5. Air fry for 20 minutes.

Serving Suggestions: Garnish with chopped green onion.

Preparation & Cooking Tips: Add a pinch of cayenne pepper to the egg mixture.

Ham & Veggie Omelette

Preparation Time: 15 minutes

Cooking Time: 10 minutes

Servings: 4

Ingredients:

- 4 eggs
- ¼ cup milk
- 2 slices ham, diced
- ¼ cup red bell pepper, diced
- ¼ cup mushrooms
- Salt to taste
- ¼ cup cheddar cheese, shredded cheese
- 1 teaspoon garden herb breakfast seasoning

Method:

1. Beat the eggs in a bowl.
2. Stir in milk, ham and veggies.
3. Season with salt.
4. Pour into a small cake pan.
5. Place pan inside the Innsky Air Fryer Oven.
6. Air fry 350 degrees F for 10 minutes.
7. Sprinkle cheese and breakfast seasoning on top.

Serving Suggestions: Serve with toasted bread.

Preparation & Cooking Tips: Use a thin spatula to loosen the egg from the pan.

Breakfast Bombs

Preparation Time: 20 minutes

Cooking Time: 10 minutes

Servings: 2

Ingredients:

- 3 eggs, cooked
- 3 slices bacon, cooked crisp and crumbled
- 1 tablespoon chives, chopped
- 1 oz. cream cheese
- 4 oz. pizza dough
- Cooking spray

Method:

1. Add eggs, bacon, chives and cream cheese to a bowl.
2. Mix well.
3. Divide pizza dough into 4.
4. Roll to form a circle.
5. Add egg mixture on top of each of portion.
6. Wrap and seal.
7. Add breakfast bombs to the air fryer oven.
8. Spray with oil.
9. Air fry at 350 degrees for 10 minutes.

Serving Suggestions: Serve with marinara dip.

Preparation & Cooking Tips: You can double the recipe but be sure to cook in batches to avoid overcrowding.

Breakfast Casserole

Preparation Time: 10 minutes

Cooking Time: 15 minutes

Servings: 4

Ingredients:

- 1 teaspoon olive oil
- ¼ cup white onion, diced
- 1 green bell pepper, diced
- 1 lb. ground sausage
- Cooking spray
- ½ cup Colby Jack cheese, shredded
- 8 eggs, beaten
- ½ teaspoon garlic salt
- 1 teaspoon fennel seed

Method:

1. Add olive oil to a pan over medium heat.
2. Cook onion, bell pepper and sausage until sausage is browned.
3. Spray a small baking pan with oil.
4. Add the sausage mixture to the pan.
5. Top with cheese and then with the eggs.
6. Season with garlic salt and fennel seed.
7. Air fry at 390 degrees F for 15 minutes.

Serving Suggestions: Sprinkle with chopped chives before serving.

Preparation & Cooking Tips: You can also use turkey sausage for this recipe.

Breakfast Sausage

Preparation Time: 10 minutes

Cooking Time: 20 minutes

Servings: 8

Ingredients:

- 1 lb. ground turkey
- 1 lb. ground pork
- 1 tablespoon maple syrup
- 2 teaspoons garlic powder
- 2 teaspoons dry rubbed sage
- 2 teaspoons fennel seeds
- 1 teaspoon dried thyme
- 1 teaspoon paprika
- Salt to taste

Method:

1. In a bowl, mix all the ingredients.
2. Form patties from the mixture.
3. Place the patties in the Innsky Air Fryer Oven.
4. Cook at 370 degrees F for 10 to 20 minutes.

Serving Suggestions: Serve with toasted bread.

Preparation & Cooking Tips: Cook in batches.

Breakfast Pockets

Preparation Time: 20 minutes

Cooking Time: 10 minutes

Servings: 4

Ingredients:

- 1 pack puff pastry sheets
- 5 eggs, beaten and cooked
- ½ cup breakfast sausage, cooked and crumbled
- ½ cup cheddar cheese, shredded
- ½ cup bacon, cooked and chopped

Method:

1. Cut rectangles from the pastry sheets.
2. In a bowl, mix the remaining ingredients.
3. Add mixture on top of the sheets.
4. Place another pastry sheet on top.
5. Seal the edges by pressing together using a fork.
6. Add breakfast pockets to the Innsky Air Fryer Oven.
7. Cook at 370 degrees F for 5 to 10 minutes.

Serving Suggestions: Serve with garden salad.

Preparation & Cooking Tips: Check every 3 minutes.

French Toast

Preparation Time: 5 minutes

Cooking Time: 12 minutes

Servings: 2

Ingredients:

- 2 tablespoons butter
- 4 pieces bread
- 2 eggs, beaten
- Pinch salt
- ¼ teaspoon ground cloves
- Pinch nutmeg
- Pinch cinnamon

Method:

1. Preheat your Innsky Air Fryer Oven to 350 degrees F.
2. Spread butter on top side of the bread.
3. Slice into strips.
4. In a bowl, mix eggs, salt and spices.
5. Dip bread strips in the mixture.
6. Place in the air fryer and cook for 2 minutes per side.

Serving Suggestions: Garnish with maple syrup.

Preparation & Cooking Tips: Use day-old bread for best results.

Breakfast Potatoes

Preparation Time: 20 minutes

Cooking Time: 25 minutes

Servings: 4

Ingredients:

- 1 ½ lb. potatoes, diced
- ½ onion, chopped
- 1 green bell pepper, chopped
- 2 cloves garlic, minced
- 1 tablespoon olive oil
- Salt and pepper to taste

Method:

1. Add all the ingredients to the air fryer basket.
2. Toss to mix.
3. Cook at 390 degrees F for 25 minutes, shaking every 8 minutes.

Serving Suggestions: Sprinkle with chopped parsley.

Preparation & Cooking Tips: Add a pinch of paprika to make it more flavorful.

Breakfast Egg Rolls

Preparation Time: 15 minutes

Cooking Time: 10 minutes

Servings: 4

Ingredients:

- ½ tablespoon olive oil
- 2 eggs
- 2 tablespoons milk
- Salt and pepper to taste
- 2 sausage patties, cooked and chopped
- ½ cup cheddar cheese, shredded
- 6 egg roll wrappers

Method:

1. Add olive oil to a pan over medium heat.
2. Beat the eggs and milk in a bowl.
3. Season with salt and pepper.
4. Add egg mixture to the pan and cook.
5. Transfer to a plate and let cool.
6. Add eggs, sausage and cheese on top of the egg roll wrappers.
7. Roll up and seal.
8. Cook in the air fryer at 400 degrees F for 4 to 5 minutes per side.

Serving Suggestions: Serve with sweet chili dipping sauce.

Preparation & Cooking Tips: You can make the rolls ahead of time and freeze for cooking later.

Baked Egg Cups

Preparation Time: 5 minutes

Cooking Time: 10 minutes

Servings: 4

Ingredients:

- 4 eggs, beaten
- ¼ cup milk
- ¼ cup spinach, sautéed and chopped
- 2 teaspoons cheddar cheese, grated
- Salt and pepper to taste

Method:

1. Mix all the ingredients in a bowl.
2. Pour into muffin cups.
3. Air fry at 330 degrees F for 12 minutes.

Serving Suggestions: Garnish with chopped herbs.

Preparation & Cooking Tips: You can also use individual ramekins instead of muffin cups.

Chapter 3: Chicken Recipes

Chicken Breast

Preparation Time: 5 minutes

Cooking Time: 20 minutes

Servings: 4

Ingredients:

- ½ teaspoon garlic powder
- ½ teaspoon dried oregano
- Salt and pepper to taste
- Cooking spray
- 4 chicken breast fillets

Method:

1. In a bowl, mix garlic powder, dried oregano, salt and pepper.
2. Spray chicken breasts with oil.
3. Sprinkle with the spice mixture.
4. Air fry at 360 degrees F for 20 minutes, flipping every 5 minutes.

Serving Suggestions: Let rest for 5 minutes before slicing and serving.

Preparation & Cooking Tips: You can replace oregano with parsley or basil.

Fried Chicken

Preparation Time: 8 hours and 20 minutes

Cooking Time: 30 minutes

Servings: 4

Ingredients:

- Cooking spray

Marinade

- 2 lb. chicken
- 1 cup buttermilk
- ¼ cup hot sauce
- 1 teaspoon paprika
- 1 teaspoon garlic powder
- Salt and pepper to taste

Breading

- 1 ½ cups flour
- 1 teaspoon paprika
- 1 teaspoon onion powder
- 1 teaspoon garlic powder
- Salt and pepper to taste

Method:

1. Mix marinade ingredients.
2. Add chicken and marinate in the refrigerator for 8 hours.
3. Preheat your air fryer oven to 375 degrees F.

4. In a bowl, mix the breading ingredients.

5. Dredge chicken with the flour mixture.

6. Place in the air fryer oven.

7. Cook for 30 minutes, flipping every 10 minutes

Serving Suggestions: Serve with ketchup and hot sauce.

Preparation & Cooking Tips: You can make this ahead of time and freeze for later cooking.

Crispy Chicken Thighs

Preparation Time: 5 minutes

Cooking Time: 25 minutes

Servings: 4

Ingredients:

- ½ cup all-purpose flour
- 1 ½ tablespoons Old Bay Cajun Seasoning
- Salt to taste
- 1 egg, beaten
- 4 chicken thighs
- Cooking spray

Method:

1. Preheat your Innsky Air Fryer Oven to 390 degrees F.
2. Mix the flour, Old Bay seasoning and salt.
3. Whisk together the flour, salt and the Old Bay.
4. Dip the chicken in eggs and dredge with flour mixture.
5. Spray with oil.
6. Cook in the air fryer for 25 minutes, flipping twice or thrice.

Serving Suggestions: Serve with ranch dressing for dipping sauce.

Preparation & Cooking Tips: You can also use other chicken parts for this recipe.

Maple Chicken

Preparation Time: 1 hour and 10 minutes

Cooking Time: 25 minutes

Servings: 4

Ingredients:

Marinade

- 1 egg, beaten
- 1 cup buttermilk
- 1 teaspoon granulated garlic
- ½ cup maple syrup
- 4 chicken thighs

Breading

- ¼ cup tapioca flour
- ½ cup all-purpose flour
- ½ teaspoon smoked paprika
- 1 teaspoon sweet paprika
- 1 teaspoon onion powder
- ½ teaspoon granulated garlic
- Pinch cayenne pepper
- Salt and pepper to taste

Method:

1. Mix marinade ingredients in a bowl.
2. Marinate chicken in the mixture for 1 hour.
3. In another bowl, combine breading ingredients.

4. Cook chicken in the air fryer at 380 degrees F for 25 minutes, flipping halfway through.

Serving Suggestions: Drizzle with maple syrup.

Preparation & Cooking Tips: Cook in batches for even browning.

Buttermilk Fried Chicken

Preparation Time: 15 minutes

Cooking Time: 20 minutes

Servings: 4

Ingredients:

- ½ teaspoon hot sauce
- 1 cup buttermilk
- ⅓ cup tapioca flour
- ½ teaspoon garlic salt
- Pepper to taste
- 1 egg, beaten
- ½ cup all-purpose flour
- ½ teaspoon paprika
- 1 ½ teaspoons brown sugar
- 1 teaspoon garlic powder
- ¼ teaspoon oregano
- ½ teaspoon onion powder
- 1 lb. chicken thighs

Method:

1. In the first bowl, mix hot sauce and buttermilk.
2. In the second bowl, combine the flour, garlic salt and pepper.
3. In the third bowl, beat the egg.
4. In the fourth bowl, mix the remaining ingredients.
5. Dip the chicken in the first, second, third and fourth bowls.
6. Cook in the air fryer at 380 degrees F for 10 minutes per side.

Serving Suggestions: Serve the chicken with a mixture of mayo and ketchup.

Preparation & Cooking Tips: Freeze the chicken for later cooking.

Chicken Tenderloin

Preparation Time: 15 minutes

Cooking Time: 20 minutes

Servings: 4

Ingredients:

- 1 egg
- 2 tablespoons vegetable oil
- ½ cup breadcrumbs
- 8 chicken tenderloins

Method:

1. Preheat your air fryer to 350 degrees F.
2. Beat the egg in a bowl.
3. Combine the oil and breadcrumbs in another bowl.
4. Dip the chicken tenderloins in the egg, and then in the crumb mixture.
5. Air fry for 6 to 8 minutes per side.

Serving Suggestions: Serve with hot sauce and mustard.

Preparation & Cooking Tips: You can also use chicken breast fillet and slice into strips.

Blackened Chicken

Preparation Time: 15 minutes

Cooking Time: 20 minutes

Servings: 4

Ingredients:

- Salt and pepper to taste
- 1 teaspoon ground thyme
- ½ teaspoon onion powder
- 2 teaspoons paprika
- ½ teaspoon cayenne pepper
- 1 teaspoon cumin
- 2 teaspoons vegetable oil
- 2 chicken breast fillets

Method:

1. Mix salt, pepper and spices in a bowl.
2. Coat chicken with oil.
3. Sprinkle both sides with spice mixture.
4. Let sit for 15 minutes.
5. Preheat your Innsky Air Fryer Oven to 360 degrees F.
6. Add the chicken to the air fryer.
7. Cook for 10 minutes per side.

Serving Suggestions: Let rest for 5 minutes before slicing and serving.

Preparation & Cooking Tips: You can also use chicken tenderloins for this recipe.

Sesame Chicken

Preparation Time: 5 minutes

Cooking Time: 15 minutes

Servings: 4

Ingredients:

- 2 tablespoons sesame oil
- 1 tablespoon sriracha sauce
- 1 tablespoon honey
- 1 teaspoon rice vinegar
- 2 tablespoons soy sauce
- 2 lb. chicken thighs

Method:

1. Mix sesame oil, sriracha sauce, honey, vinegar and soy sauce in a bowl.
2. Coat chicken with the mixture.
3. Marinate in the refrigerator for 30 minutes.
4. Preheat your air fryer to 400 degrees F.
5. Air fry chicken for 5 minutes.
6. Turn and cook for another 10 minutes.

Serving Suggestions: Garnish with chopped green onion and sesame seeds.

Preparation & Cooking Tips: Add more sriracha sauce if you want your chicken spicier.

Chapter 4: Beef Recipes

Steak & Veggies

Preparation Time: 15 minutes

Cooking Time: 4 hours and 30 minutes

Servings: 4

Ingredients:

- 1 lb. rib eye steak, sliced thinly
- 1 tablespoon low-sodium soy sauce
- 2 tablespoons Worcestershire sauce
- 1 onion, sliced
- 4 oz. mushrooms, sliced
- ½ green bell pepper, sliced thinly
- Salt and pepper to taste
- ½ teaspoon ground mustard
- 1 tablespoon olive oil

Method:

1. Add steak to a bowl.
2. Pour in soy sauce and Worcestershire sauce.
3. Cover the bowl.
4. Refrigerate for 4 hours.
5. Preheat your Innsky Air Fryer Oven ot 380 degrees F.
6. In a bowl, mix onion, bell pepper and mushrooms.
7. Stir in salt, pepper, mustard and oil.
8. Toast the hoagie rolls in the air fryer for 2 minutes.

9. Transfer to a plate.

10. Add the steak to the air fryer.

11. Cook for 3 minutes.

12. Stir and cook for 1 minute.

13. Transfer to a plate.

14. Cook vegetable mixture for 5 minutes.

15. Stir and cook for another 5 minutes.

16. Top hoagie rolls with beef and veggies.

Serving Suggestions: Drizzle cheese sauce on top.

Preparation & Cooking Tips: You can also use beef tenderloin strips for this recipe.

Beef Tenderloin

Preparation Time: 10 minutes

Cooking Time: 30 minutes

Servings: 8

Ingredients:

- 2 lb. beef tenderloin
- 1 tablespoon vegetable oil
- Salt and pepper to taste
- 1 teaspoon dried oregano

Method:

1. Preheat your Innsky Air Fryer to 400 degrees F.
2. Drizzle beef tenderloin with oil.
3. Season with salt, pepper and oregano.
4. Place in the air fryer.
5. Air fry at 390 degrees F for 22 minutes.
6. Reduce heat to 360 degrees and cook for another 10 minutes.

Serving Suggestions: Let rest for 10 minutes before serving.

Preparation & Cooking Tips: Slice tenderloin into strips before cooking to shorten cooking time.

Rib Eye Steak

Preparation Time: 2 hours and 10 minutes

Cooking Time: 20 minutes

Servings: 2

Ingredients:

- 2 rib-eye steaks
- ¼ cup olive oil
- 4 teaspoons steak seasoning
- ½ cup low-sodium soy sauce

Method:

1. Coat steaks with oil.
2. Sprinkle both sides of steak with steak seasoning.
3. Marinate in soy sauce for 2 hours.
4. Add about 1 tablespoon water to the bottom of the air fryer pan to prevent it from smoking during the cooking process.
5. Preheat your air fryer to 400 degrees F.
6. Cook steaks to 7 minutes.
7. Flip and cook for another 7 minutes.

Serving Suggestions: Serve with mashed potatoes and gravy.

Preparation & Cooking Tips: Add a tablespoon of water to the air fryer to prevent smoking during cooking.

Steak & Mushrooms

Preparation Time: 10 minutes

Cooking Time: 20 minutes

Servings: 4

Ingredients:

- 2 tablespoons butter
- 1 lb. steaks, sliced into cubes
- 8 oz. mushrooms, sliced in half
- ½ teaspoon garlic powder
- 1 teaspoon Worcestershire sauce
- Salt and pepper to taste

Method:

1. Combine all ingredients in a bowl.
2. Preheat your Innsky Air Fry to 400 degrees F.
3. Air fry for 20 minutes, flipping once or twice.

Serving Suggestions: Drizzle with melted butter before serving.

Preparation & Cooking Tips: You can also sprinkle with chili flakes.

Meatloaf

Preparation Time: 10 minutes

Cooking Time: 25 minutes

Servings: 4

Ingredients:

- 1 tablespoon olive oil
- 1 lb. lean ground beef
- 1 onion, chopped
- 3 tablespoons breadcrumbs
- 1 tablespoon fresh thyme, chopped
- 1 egg, beaten
- 1 cup mushrooms, chopped
- Salt and pepper to taste

Method:

1. Preheat your air fryer to 392 degrees F.
2. Mix all the ingredients.
3. Press mixture onto a small loaf pan.
4. Add to the air fryer.
5. Cook for 25 minutes.

Serving Suggestions: Let rest for 10 minutes before slicing.

Preparation & Cooking Tips: You can also chopped vegetables like carrots or potatoes to the mixture.

Roast Beef

Preparation Time: 10 minutes

Cooking Time: 35 minutes

Servings: 8

Ingredients:

- 2 lb. beef roast top round
- Cooking spray

Rub

- 2 teaspoons garlic powder
- Salt and pepper to taste

Method:

1. Place the beef roast in a baking pan.
2. Spray all sides with oil.
3. Add to the air fryer oven.
4. Cook at 400 degrees F for 20 minutes.
5. Turn and cook for another 15 minutes.

Serving Suggestions: Let rest for 15 minutes before serving.

Preparation & Cooking Tips: You can also use garlic salt in place of salt and garlic powder.

Beef Tips

Preparation Time: 10 minutes

Cooking Time: 15 minutes

Servings: 4

Ingredients:

- 1 lb. rib eye steak, sliced into cubes
- 2 tablespoons coconut amino
- 1 teaspoon paprika
- 2 teaspoons onion powder
- 1 teaspoon garlic powder
- 2 teaspoons rosemary, crushed
- Salt and pepper to taste

Method:

1. Add the beef cubes to a bowl.
2. In another bowl, mix the rest of the ingredients.
3. Pour mixture into the bowl with beef.
4. Marinate for 15 minutes.
5. Add to the Innsky Air Fryer Oven.
6. Air fry at 380 degrees F for 12 minutes, flipping once.

Serving Suggestions: Drizzle with melted butter before serving.

Preparation & Cooking Tips: You can also slice the beef into strips.

Mongolian Beef

Preparation Time: 20 minutes

Cooking Time: 20 minutes

Servings: 4

Ingredients:

Meat

- 1 lb. flank steak, slice into thin strips
- ¼ cup cornstarch

Sauce

- 2 teaspoons vegetable oil
- ½ cup soy sauce
- 1 tablespoon garlic, minced
- ½ teaspoon ginger
- ¾ cup brown sugar
- ½ cup water

Method:

1. Coat both sides of steak with cornstarch.
2. Cook in the air fryer at 390 degrees F for 10 minutes per side.
3. In a pan over medium heat, cook the sauce ingredients.
4. Bring to a boil.
5. Pour the sauce over the steak strips before serving.

Serving Suggestions: Garnish with chopped green onions.

Preparation & Cooking Tips: You can also use prepared Mongolian sauce.

Chapter 5: Pork Recipes

Pork Chops

Preparation Time: 10 minutes

Cooking Time: 20 minutes

Servings: 4

Ingredients:

- ½ cup Parmesan cheese, grated
- 1 teaspoon paprika
- 1 teaspoon garlic powder
- 1 teaspoon dried parsley
- Salt and pepper to taste
- 4 pork chops
- 2 tablespoons olive oil

Method:

1. Preheat your Innsky Air Fryer Oven to 380 degrees F.
2. In a bowl, mix the Parmesan cheese, spices, salt and pepper.
3. Drizzle pork chops with oil.
4. Sprinkle both with the Parmesan mixture.
5. Cook for 10 minutes.
6. Flip and cook for another 10 minutes.

Serving Suggestions: Let rest for 5 minutes before serving.

Preparation & Cooking Tips: Use boneless pork chops for this recipe.

Breaded Pork Chops

Preparation Time: 10 minutes

Cooking Time: 10 minutes

Servings: 4

Ingredients:

- 4 pork chops
- 1 teaspoon Cajun seasoning
- 2 eggs, beaten
- 1 ½ cups breadcrumbs
- Cooking spray

Method:

1. Preheat your air fryer to 390 degrees F.
2. Sprinkle pork chops with seasoning.
3. Dip in egg and dredge with breadcrumbs.
4. Spray with oil.
5. Add to the air fryer.
6. Cook for 5 minutes per side.

Serving Suggestions: Serve with dip of choice.

Preparation & Cooking Tips: You can also make your own breading by pulsing croutons in a food processor.

Pork Chops & Broccoli

Preparation Time: 5 minutes

Cooking Time: 10 minutes

Servings: 2

Ingredients:

- 2 pork chops
- 2 5-ounce bone-in pork chops
- 2 tablespoons avocado oil, divided
- ½ teaspoon onion powder
- ½ teaspoon garlic powder
- ½ teaspoon paprika
- Salt to taste
- 2 cups broccoli florets
- 2 cloves garlic, minced

Method:

1. Preheat your Innsky Air Fryer Oven to 350 degrees F.
2. Spray your air fryer basket with oil.
3. Drizzle pork chops with half of avocado oil.
4. Sprinkle both sides with spices and salt.
5. Cook in the air fryer for 5 minutes per side.
6. In a bowl, toss the broccoli in half of oil.
7. Season with salt.
8. Add to the air fryer.
9. Cook for another 5 minutes.

Serving Suggestions: Garnish with chopped fresh herbs.

Preparation & Cooking Tips: Use bone-in pork chops for this recipe.

Spiced Pork Tenderloin

Preparation Time: 15 minutes

Cooking Time: 30 minutes

Servings: 4

Ingredients:

Pork

- 1 tablespoon olive oil
- 1 (1 1/2 pound) pork tenderloin, trimmed

Rub

- 1 tablespoon smoked paprika
- 1 teaspoon ground mustard
- ¼ teaspoon ground cayenne pepper
- ¼ teaspoon garlic powder
- 2 tablespoons brown sugar
- Salt and pepper to taste

Method:

1. Mix the rub ingredients in a bowl.
2. Brush both sides of pork with oil.
3. Sprinkle with spice mixture.
4. Marinate for 5 minutes.
5. Preheat your air fryer to 400 degrees F.
6. Cook in the air fryer for 20 minutes, flipping once.

Serving Suggestions: Garnish with crispy garlic slivers.

Preparation & Cooking Tips: You can also use pork chops for this recipe.

Sweet & Sour Pork

Preparation Time: 10 minutes

Cooking Time: 20 minutes

Servings: 4

Ingredients:

- 1 ½ lb. pork cutlets, sliced into cubes
- 1 teaspoon sesame oil
- 3 tablespoons cornstarch

Sauce

- ¼ cup rice vinegar
- ¼ cup white sugar
- 2 tablespoons soy sauce
- 4 tablespoons ketchup

Method:

1. Toss the pork cutlets in oil and cornstarch.
2. Preheat your air fryer oven to 350 degrees F.
3. Cook pork cutlets for 10 minutes per side.
4. Heat the sauce ingredients in a pan over medium high heat.
5. Pour sauce over the pork cutlets and serve.

Serving Suggestions: Garnish with chopped chives.

Preparation & Cooking Tips: You can also add vegetables like steamed carrots and bell pepper to the mixture.

Mustard Pork

Preparation Time: 10 minutes

Cooking Time: 30 minutes

Servings: 4

Ingredients:

- 2 tablespoons brown sugar
- ¼ cup Dijon mustard
- ½ teaspoon dried thyme
- 1 teaspoon dried parsley flakes
- Salt and pepper to taste
- 1 ¼ lb. pork tenderloin
- 1 tablespoon olive oil

Method:

1. Preheat your air fryer to 400 degrees F.
2. Combine the brown sugar, mustard, thyme, parsley, salt and pepper in a bowl.
3. Stir in the pork.
4. Coat evenly with the mixture.
5. Cook in the air fryer for 20 minutes.
6. Flip and cook for another 10 minutes.

Serving Suggestions: Serve with steamed beans and potatoes.

Preparation & Cooking Tips: You can also marinate in the mixture for 30 minutes.

Pork Belly Bites

Preparation Time: 15 minutes

Cooking Time: 15 minutes

Servings: 4

Ingredients:

- 1 lb. pork belly
- ½ teaspoon garlic powder
- 1 teaspoon Worcestershire sauce
- Salt and pepper to taste

Method:

1. Preheat your air fryer to 400 degrees F.
2. Mix all the ingredients.
3. Place in the air fryer oven.
4. Cook for 20 minutes, flipping twice.

Serving Suggestions: Serve warm.

Preparation & Cooking Tips: Remove the skin from the pork belly.

Korean Pork

Preparation Time: 10 minutes

Cooking Time: 20 minutes

Servings: 6

Ingredients:

- 3 lb. pork ribs
- ¼ cup sesame oil
- 1 cup soy sauce
- 5 cloves, garlic
- 1/3 cup brown sugar

Method:

1. Combine all the ingredients in a bowl.
2. Marinate for 2 hours.
3. Air fry the pork ribs at 400 degrees F for 20 minutes, flipping twice.

Serving Suggestions: Garnish with chopped chives and sesame seeds.

Preparation & Cooking Tips: You can also add vegetables to the mixture.

Chapter 6: Seafood Recipes

Shrimp with Spicy Remoulade Sauce

Preparation Time: 15 minutes

Cooking Time: 10 minutes

Servings: 4

Ingredients:

Shrimp

- 1 lb. shrimp, peeled and deveined
- ½ cup all-purpose flour
- Salt and pepper to taste
- 2 eggs, beaten
- 1 cup breadcrumbs

Sauce

- 1 tablespoon ketchup
- ½ cup mayonnaise
- 2 tablespoons mustard
- 2 tablespoons pickled jalapenos, chopped
- 1 scallion, chopped
- 1 tablespoon hot sauce

Method:

1. Mix flour, salt and pepper in a bowl.
2. Add eggs to another bowl, and breadcrumbs to a third bowl.
3. Coat shrimp with the flour mixture.

4. Dip in eggs and dredge with breadcrumbs.

5. Air fry at 385 degrees F for 5 minutes per side.

6. Mix the sauce ingredients in a bowl.

7. Serve shrimp with the sauce.

Serving Suggestions: Garnish shrimp with chopped green onion.

Preparation & Cooking Tips: Cook shrimp in batches.

Lobster Tails

Preparation Time: 5 minutes

Cooking Time: 10 minutes

Servings: 4

Ingredients:

- 4 lobster tails
- 2 tablespoons butter, melted
- Salt and pepper to taste
- Instructions

Method:

1. Preheat your Innsky Air Fryer Oven to 380 degrees F.
2. Slice the lobster in the tail section using kitchen shears.
3. Pull back the lobster shell.
4. Brush the lobster flesh with butter.
5. Season with salt and pepper.
6. Cook in the air fryer at 380 degrees F for 10 minutes.

Serving Suggestions: Sprinkle with chopped parsley.

Preparation & Cooking Tips: You can also use frozen lobster tails for this recipe. Just add 5 to 10 minutes

Tuna Patties

Preparation Time: 2 hours and 10 minutes

Cooking Time: 15 minutes

Servings: 4

Ingredients:

- 2 cups tuna flakes
- 1 tablespoon lemon juice
- 2 teaspoons Dijon mustard
- ½ cup breadcrumbs
- 3 tablespoons olive oil
- 1 egg, beaten
- 2 tablespoons parsley, chopped
- Salt and pepper to taste

Method:

1. Combine all the ingredients in a bowl.
2. Form patties from the mixture.
3. Cover and refrigerate patties for 2 hours.
4. Preheat your Innsky Air Fryer Oven to 360 degrees F.
5. Add to the air fryer.
6. Cook for 10 minutes.

Serving Suggestions: Serve with hot pepper sauce.

Preparation & Cooking Tips: Cook for another 5 minutes to make it crispier.

Lemon Pepper Shrimp

Preparation Time: 10 minutes

Cooking Time: 10 minutes

Servings: 2

Ingredients:

- 1 tablespoon olive oil
- 1 tablespoon lemon juice
- ¼ teaspoon paprika
- ¼ teaspoon garlic powder
- 1 teaspoon lemon pepper
- 12 oz. shrimp, peeled and deveined

Method:

1. Preheat your air fryer to 400 degrees F.
2. In a bowl, mix the oil, lemon juice and spices.
3. Stir in the shrimp.
4. Coat evenly with the sauce.
5. Add shrimp to the air fryer.
6. Cook for 10 minutes, flipping once.

Serving Suggestions: Garnish with lemon slices.

Preparation & Cooking Tips: You can also use frozen shrimp for this recipe.

Fish Sticks

Preparation Time: 10 minutes

Cooking Time: 5 minutes

Servings: 4

Ingredients:

- 1 lb. cod fillets, sliced into strips
- ½ cup all-purpose flour
- 1 egg, beaten
- ½ cup breadcrumbs
- ½ teaspoon lemon-pepper seasoning
- ½ teaspoon paprika
- Salt and pepper to taste
- Cooking spray

Method:

1. Coat the cod strips with flour.
2. Dip in egg.
3. Mix breadcrumbs, paprika, salt and pepper.
4. Dredge fish strips with this mixture.
5. Arrange fish sticks in the air fryer.
6. Spray with oil.
7. Air fry at 400 degrees F for 5 minutes.

Serving Suggestions: Serve with sweet chili sauce.

Preparation & Cooking Tips: For extra crispy results, cook for another 5 minutes.

Cajun Shrimp

Preparation Time: 10 minutes

Cooking Time: 10 minutes

Servings: 4

Ingredients:

- 1 tablespoon Cajun seasoning
- 24 shrimp, peeled and deveined
- 1 red bell pepper, sliced
- 1 zucchini, sliced
- 2 tablespoons olive oil
- 6 oz. turkey sausage, cooked
- Salt to taste

Method:

1. Coat shrimp with Cajun seasoning.
2. Stir in the rest of the ingredients.
3. Preheat your air fryer to 400 degrees F.
4. Cook shrimp mixture for 10 minutes, stirring twice.

Serving Suggestions: Garnish with chopped green onions.

Preparation & Cooking Tips: You can also use pork sausage for this recipe.

Garlic Parmesan Salmon

Preparation Time: 10 minutes

Cooking Time: 15 minutes

Servings: 4

Ingredients:

- Cooking spray
- 4 salmon fillets
- Pepper to taste
- ½ teaspoon Italian seasoning
- ¼ cup Parmesan cheese, shredded
- ¼ cup breadcrumbs
- 2 tablespoons butter, melted
- 2 cloves garlic, minced

Method:

1. Preheat your air fryer to 400 degrees F.
2. Spray both sides of fish with oil.
3. Season with pepper.
4. In a bowl, mix the Italian seasoning, Parmesan cheese and breadcrumbs.
5. Dredge salmon fillets with this mixture.
6. Cook in the air fryer for 15 minutes.
7. In a pan over medium heat, add the butter and garlic.
8. Cook for 1 minute, stirring often.
9. Pour butter mixture over the salmon and serve.

Serving Suggestions: Garnish with crispy garlic bits.

Preparation & Cooking Tips: You can also slice salmon into strips.

Lemon Garlic Salmon

Preparation Time: 30 minutes

Cooking Time: 25 minutes

Servings: 4

Ingredients:

- 4 salmon fillets
- 2 tablespoons olive oil
- 1 teaspoon lemon juice
- 2 teaspoons Italian seasoning
- 2 teaspoons garlic powder
- Salt and pepper to taste

Method:

1. Marinate salmon fillets in a mixture of olive oil and lemon juice for 15 minutes.
2. Sprinkle both sides of Italian seasoning, garlic powder, salt and pepper.
3. Arrange salmon fillets in the air fryer oven.
4. Cook at 400 degrees F for 10 minutes.
5. Flip and cook for another 15 minutes.

Serving Suggestions: Garnish with lemon slices.

Preparation & Cooking Tips: You can also dredge the salmon with breadcrumbs to make it crispier.

Chapter 7: Snack Recipes

Potato Chips

Preparation Time: 5 minutes

Cooking Time: 15 minutes

Servings: 4

Ingredients:

- 1 potato, sliced
- 1 tablespoon vegetable oil
- Salt and pepper to taste
- 1 teaspoon rosemary, chopped

Method:

1. Coat potato slices with oil.
2. Season with salt and pepper.
3. Add to the air fryer.
4. Cook at 375 degrees F for 15 minutes.
5. Sprinkle with chopped rosemary before serving.

Serving Suggestions: Serve right away or store in airtight containers for up to 3 days.

Preparation & Cooking Tips: Potato slices should be 1/8 inch thick.

Sweet Potato Tots

Preparation Time: 15 minutes

Cooking Time: 30 minutes

Servings: 4

Ingredients:

- 2 sweet potatoes, peeled
- Water
- Salt to taste
- 1/8 teaspoon garlic powder
- 1 tablespoon potato starch
- Cooking spray

Method:

1. Boil sweet potatoes in a pot of water.
2. Cook for 15 minutes.
3. Transfer to a plate.
4. Grate sweet potatoes.
5. Mix with the rest of the ingredients.
6. Form cylinders from the mixture.
7. Spray with oil.
8. Add to the Innsky Air Fryer Oven.
9. Air fry at 400 degrees F for 15 minutes, flipping once or twice.

Serving Suggestions: Serve with ketchup.

Preparation & Cooking Tips: You can also use flour instead of potato starch.

Banana Bread

Preparation Time: 15 minutes

Cooking Time: 45 minutes

Servings: 8

Ingredients:

- Cooking spray

Dry ingredients

- ¾ cup whole wheat flour
- ¼ teaspoon baking soda
- ½ cup sugar
- 1 teaspoon cinnamon
- Pinch salt

Wet ingredients

- 2 ripe bananas, mashed
- 1/3 cup yogurt
- 2 eggs, beaten
- 2 tablespoons vegetable oil
- 1 teaspoon vanilla extract

Topping

- 2 tablespoons walnuts, toasted and chopped

Method:

1. Spray a small cake pan with oil.

2. In a bowl, mix the dry ingredients.

3. In another bowl, whisk the wet ingredients.

4. Add the first bowl to the second bowl.

5. Pour mixture into the cake pan.

6. Top with the walnuts.

7. Air fry at 310 degrees F for 30 minutes.

Serving Suggestions: Let cool for 15 minutes before inverting pan and slicing.

Preparation & Cooking Tips: Insert a toothpick into the bread. If it comes out clean, it means that it is done.

Avocado Fries

Preparation Time: 15 minutes

Cooking Time: 15 minutes

Servings: 4

Ingredients:

- Pepper to taste
- ½ cup all-purpose flour
- 2 eggs
- 1 tablespoon water
- ½ cup breadcrumbs
- 2 avocados, sliced into wedges
- Cooking spray

Method:

1. Combine pepper and flour in a bowl.
2. Beat eggs in another bowl.
3. Stir in water.
4. Add breadcrumbs to a third bowl.
5. Coat the avocado wedges with flour mixture.
6. Dip in eggs and dredge with breadcrumbs.
7. Spray with oil.
8. Add to the Innsky Air Fryer Oven.
9. Cook at 400 degrees F for 10 minutes, flipping once.

Serving Suggestions: Serve with a mixture of mayo and ketchup for dipping sauce.

Preparation & Cooking Tips: Season with a pinch of salt.

Empanada

Preparation Time: 20 minutes

Cooking Time: 10 minutes

Servings: 4

Ingredients:

- 1 tablespoon olive oil
- ¼ cup white onion, chopped
- 3 oz. lean ground beef
- 2 teaspoons garlic, chopped
- 6 olives, pitted and chopped
- 3 oz. mushrooms, chopped
- ¼ teaspoon ground cumin
- ¼ teaspoon paprika
- 1/8 teaspoon ground cinnamon
- 8 gyoza wrappers
- 1 egg, beaten

Method:

1. In a pan over medium heat, add the oil and cook onion and beef for 3 minutes.
2. Stir in the rest of the ingredients except wrappers and eggs.
3. Cook for 5 minutes, stirring often.
4. Transfer to a bowl. Let cool.
5. Add mixture on top of the wrappers.
6. Fold and seal edges by brushing with egg.
7. Add the empanadas to the air fryer.
8. Cook at 400 degrees F for 7 to 10 minutes or until golden.

Serving Suggestions: Serve with coffee or tea.

Preparation & Cooking Tips: You can also freeze the cooked empanadas and reheat when ready to serve.

Whole Wheat Pizza

Preparation Time: 10 minutes

Cooking Time: 5 minutes

Servings: 2

Ingredients:

- ¼ cup marinara sauce
- 2 whole-wheat pita
- 1 oz. mozzarella cheese, shredded
- 1 clove garlic, minced
- 1 tomato, sliced
- 1 cup baby spinach
- 1 tablespoon Parmesan cheese

Method:

1. Spread a layer of marina sauce on top of the pita bread.
2. Top with the cheese, garlic, tomato and spinach.
3. Cook in the air fryer at 350 degrees F for 5 minutes.
4. Sprinkle with Parmesan cheese.

Serving Suggestions: You can also drizzle with ranch dressing before serving.

Preparation & Cooking Tips: You can also include fresh basil as topping.

Mexican Corn

Preparation Time: 10 minutes

Cooking Time: 15 minutes

Servings: 4

Ingredients:

- 4 ears fresh corn, shucked
- Cooking spray
- 1 ½ tablespoons butter
- 2 teaspoons garlic, chopped
- 1 tablespoon lime juice
- 1 teaspoon lime zest
- Salt and pepper to taste

Method:

1. Spray corn with oil.
2. Air fry at 400 degrees F for 15 minutes, turning once halfway through.
3. In a pan over medium heat, melt the butter.
4. Stir in garlic, lime juice, lime zest, salt and pepper.
5. Pour butter mixture over corn.

Serving Suggestions: Garnish with fresh cilantro.

Preparation & Cooking Tips: You can also make the same recipe using corn kernels.

Sweet Potato Fries

Preparation Time: 15 minutes

Cooking Time: 15 minutes

Servings: 4

Ingredients:

- 1 tablespoon olive oil
- ¼ teaspoon garlic powder
- 1 teaspoon thyme, chopped
- Salt to taste
- 2 sweet potatoes, sliced into strips
- Cooking spray

Method:

1. Combine oil, garlic powder, thyme and salt in a bowl.
2. Coat sweet potatoes with this mixture.
3. Add sweet potatoes to the Innsky Air Fryer Oven.
4. Air fry at 400 degrees F for 15 minutes, flipping once halfway through.

Serving Suggestions: Serve with ketchup.

Preparation & Cooking Tips: Soak the sweet potatoes in water for 10 minutes and dry thoroughly with paper towels before coating with oil mixture.

Chapter 8: Appetizer Recipes

Italian Meatballs

Preparation Time: 10 minutes

Cooking Time: 12 minutes

Servings: 6

Ingredients:

- 2 tablespoons olive oil
- 1 shallot, minced
- 3 cloves garlic, minced
- ¼ cup breadcrumbs
- 2 tablespoons milk
- 2/3 lb. lean ground beef
- ¼ lb. turkey sausage
- 1 egg, beaten
- ¼ cup parsley, chopped
- 1 tablespoon rosemary, chopped
- 1 tablespoon thyme, chopped
- 1 tablespoon mustard
- Salt to taste

Method:

1. Preheat your air fryer to 400 degrees F.
2. Add oil to a pan over medium heat.
3. Cook shallots for 1 minute.
4. Stir in garlic and cook for another 1 minute.

5. Turn off heat.

6. Add cooked shallots and garlic to a bowl.

7. Stir in the rest of the ingredients.

8. Form meatballs from the mixture.

9. Add meatballs to the air fryer.

10. Cook at 400 degrees F for 10 minutes.

Serving Suggestions: Serve with toothpicks as appetizer.

Preparation & Cooking Tips: You can also make these meatballs as topping for pasta.

Chicken Wing Appetizer

Preparation Time: 10 minutes

Cooking Time: 40 minutes

Servings: 4 to 6

Ingredients:

- 12 chicken wings
- Cooking spray
- 1 teaspoon garlic, minced
- ½ teaspoon ginger, minced
- 1 tablespoon soy sauce
- 2 teaspoons honey
- ½ teaspoon cornstarch
- 1 teaspoon lime juice
- 1 teaspoon Thai chili paste
- Salt to taste

Method:

1. Spray chicken with oil.
2. Air fry at 400 degrees F for 25 minutes, turning once halfway through.
3. In a pan over medium heat, combine the remaining ingredients.
4. Bring to a boil.
5. Reduce heat and simmer for 10 minutes.
6. Coat chicken wings with the sauce and serve.

Serving Suggestions: Garnish with chopped scallions.

Preparation & Cooking Tips: You can also use chicken drumettes for this recipe.

Spanakopita Bites

Preparation Time: 15 minutes

Cooking Time: 12 minutes

Servings: 8

Ingredients:

- 4 phyllo dough sheets
- Cooking spray
- ¼ cup feta cheese, crumbled
- ¼ cup cottage cheese
- 10 oz. baby spinach, steamed
- Salt and pepper to taste
- 1 egg white, beaten
- 2 tablespoons Parmesan cheese, grated
- 1 teaspoon dried oregano
- 1 teaspoon lemon zest

Method:

1. Spray dough sheets with oil.
2. In a bowl, combine the rest of the ingredients.
3. Top each sheet with the mixture.
4. Fold into a triangle and seal the edges.
5. Spray each triangle with oil.
6. Add to the air fryer basket.
7. Cook at 375 degrees F for 12 minutes, turning once halfway through.

Serving Suggestions: Serve immediately or let cool for 5 minutes.

Preparation & Cooking Tips: You can freeze spanakopita bites and reheat when ready to serve.

Buffalo Cauliflower Bites

Preparation Time: 10 minutes

Cooking Time: 20 minutes

Servings: 4

Ingredients:

- 1 egg white
- 2 tablespoons hot sauce
- 3 tablespoons ketchup
- ¾ cup breadcrumbs
- 4 cups cauliflower florets
- Cooking spray
- 1 tablespoon blue cheese, crumbled
- ¼ cup sour cream
- 1 teaspoon red wine vinegar
- 1 clove garlic, minced
- Pepper to taste

Method:

1. Mix egg white, hot sauce and ketchup in a bowl.
2. Add breadcrumbs to another bowl.
3. Coat cauliflower florets with egg white mixture and dredge with breadcrumbs.
4. Spray with oil.
5. Air fry at 320 degrees F for 20 minutes.
6. Mix the remaining ingredients in a bowl.
7. Serve cauliflower bites with sour cream sauce.

Serving Suggestions: Garnish with chopped parsley.

Preparation & Cooking Tips: Cook in batches.

Spicy Chicken Wings

Preparation Time: 20 minutes

Cooking Time: 45 minutes

Servings: 5

Ingredients:

- 10 chicken wings
- Cooking spray
- 1 tablespoon toasted sesame oil
- 1 clove garlic, minced
- 2 tablespoons chicken stock
- ¼ cup rice vinegar
- 3 tablespoons honey
- 1 tablespoon soy sauce
- 1 teaspoon red pepper flakes

Method:

1. Add chicken to the air fryer basket.
2. Spray with oil.
3. Air fry at 400 degrees F for 30 minutes, flipping once or twice.
4. Combine the remaining ingredients in a pan over medium heat.
5. Cook until sauce is reduced and thickened.
6. Coat chicken with mixture and serve.

Serving Suggestions: Garnish with chopped chives and roasted peanuts.

Preparation & Cooking Tips: Freeze air fried chicken. Reheat and coat with mixture when ready to serve.

Goat Cheese Balls

Preparation Time: 10 minutes

Cooking Time: 5 minutes

Servings: 24

Ingredients:

- 8 oz. goat cheese
- 2 tablespoons flour
- 1 egg, beaten
- ½ cup breadcrumbs
- ¼ cup honey

Method:

1. Divide goat cheese into 24 balls.
2. Coat each ball with flour.
3. Dip in egg and dredge with breadcrumbs.
4. Air fry at 390 degrees For 5 minutes.
5. Drizzle with honey before serving.

Serving Suggestions: You can also sprinkle with Parmesan cheese.

Preparation & Cooking Tips: Freeze goat cheese for 1 hour to make it easier to divide.

Chickpeas

Preparation Time: 5 minutes

Cooking Time: 20 minutes

Servings: 4

Ingredients:

- 19 oz. canned chickpeas
- 1 tablespoon olive oil
- ¼ teaspoon garlic powder
- ¼ teaspoon onion powder
- ½ teaspoon paprika
- Salt to taste

Method:

1. Preheat your air fryer to 390 degrees F.
2. Toss the chickpeas in oil.
3. Sprinkle with spices.
4. Place in the air fryer.
5. Cook for 15 minutes.
6. Stir and cook for another 5 minutes.

Serving Suggestions: Adjust seasoning before serving.

Preparation & Cooking Tips: Store in an airtight container.

Crispy Onion Rings

Preparation Time: 10 minutes

Cooking Time: 10 minutes

Servings: 4

Ingredients:

- ¼ teaspoon paprika
- ½ cup all-purpose flour
- Salt to taste
- 1 egg, beaten
- 1 tablespoon water
- 1 cup breadcrumbs
- 1 sweet onion, sliced into thick rings
- Cooking spray
- ¼ cup Greek yogurt
- 1 tablespoon ketchup
- 2 tablespoons mayonnaise
- ¼ teaspoon garlic powder
- 1 teaspoon mustard

Method:

1. In a bowl, mix paprika, flour and salt.
2. Add beaten egg to another bowl.
3. Stir in water.
4. Add breadcrumbs to a third bowl.
5. Coat onion rings with flour mixture.
6. Dip in the egg wash and cover with breadcrumbs.

7. Spray with oil.

8. Air fry at 375 degrees F for 10 minutes, turning once.

9. Mix the remaining ingredients in a bowl.

10. Serve with the onion rings.

Serving Suggestions: Garnish with chopped parsley.

Preparation & Cooking Tips: Use nonfat plain Greek yogurt for the dip.

Beet Chips

Preparation Time: 15 minutes

Cooking Time: 15 minutes

Servings: 4

Ingredients:

- 3 beets, sliced
- 2 teaspoons vegetable oil
- Salt and pepper to taste

Method:

1. Coat beets in oil.
2. Season with salt and pepper.
3. Air fry at 320 degrees F for 30 minutes, stirring every 10 minutes.

Serving Suggestions: Sprinkle with a little more salt if needed.

Crispy Quesadillas

Preparation Time: 20 minutes

Cooking Time: 20 minutes

Servings: 4

Ingredients:

- 4 tortillas
- 4 oz. cheddar cheese, shredded
- 1 cup red bell pepper, sliced
- 1 cup canned black beans, rinsed and drained
- 1 cup zucchini, sliced
- Cooking spray

Dip

- 2 oz. Greek yogurt
- 1 teaspoon lime zest
- 1 tablespoon lime juice
- ¼ teaspoon ground cumin
- 2 tablespoons fresh cilantro, chopped

Pico de gallo

- ¼ cup tomato, chopped
- ¼ cup cucumber, chopped
- ¼ cup white onion, chopped

Method:

1. Add the tortillas on the kitchen table.

2. Sprinkle with cheese.

3. Add red bell pepper, black beans and zucchini.

4. Fold and spray with oil.

5. Place in the air fryer.

6. Air fry at 400 degrees F for 10 minutes per side.

7. Mix the ingredients for dip and for pico de gallo in separate bowls.

8. Serve quesadillas with yogurt mixture and tomato mixture.

Serving Suggestions: Garnish with chopped chives.

Preparation & Cooking Tips: Cook 5 minutes more for extra crispy quesadillas.

Chapter 9: Side Dish Recipes

Garlic Green Beans

Preparation Time: 5 minutes

Cooking Time: 10 minutes

Servings: 4

Ingredients:

- 1 lb. green beans, trimmed
- 1 tablespoon olive oil
- Salt and pepper to taste
- 1 teaspoon garlic powder

Method:

1. Coat green beans with oil.
2. Sprinkle with salt, pepper and garlic powder.
3. Add to the air fryer basket.
4. Cook for 10 minutes, stirring once.

Serving Suggestions: You can also sprinkle with grated Parmesan cheese before serving.

Preparation & Cooking Tips: You can use minced garlic in place of garlic powder.

Cheesy Broccoli

Preparation Time: 15 minutes

Cooking Time: 13 minutes

Servings: 4

Ingredients:

- 6 cups broccoli florets
- Cooking spray
- 1 ½ oz. Mexican cheese, crumbled
- 10 tablespoons evaporated milk

Method:

1. Spray broccoli florets with oil.
2. Add to the air fryer.
3. Cook at 375 degrees F for 8 minutes, stirring once.
4. Add the cheese and milk to a saucepan over medium low heat.
5. Cook while stirring for 5 minutes.
6. Drizzle cheese sauce over broccoli florets.

Serving Suggestions: Garnish with herbs.

Preparation & Cooking Tips: Cook in batches.

Crushed Baked Potatoes

Preparation Time: 10 minutes

Cooking Time: 20 minutes

Servings: 2

Ingredients:

- 11 oz. potatoes
- 1 teaspoon olive oil
- 2 slices bacon, cooked crisp and chopped
- ½ oz. cheddar cheese, shredded
- 1 tablespoon chopped chives
- Salt to taste

Method:

1. Coat potatoes with oil.
2. Cook in the air fryer at 350 degrees F for 25 minutes, stirring at least once.
3. Transfer potatoes to a serving plate.
4. Crush potatoes.
5. Top with cheese, bacon, chives and salt.

Serving Suggestions: Serve with sour cream.

Preparation & Cooking Tips: You can also use mozzarella cheese.

Sesame Tofu

Preparation Time: 10 minutes

Cooking Time: 30 minutes

Servings: 4

Ingredients:

- 28 oz. tofu, sliced into cubes
- Cooking spray
- ¼ cup orange juice
- 2 tablespoons soy sauce
- 1 tablespoon sesame oil
- 1 tablespoon honey
- ½ teaspoon cornstarch
- 1 teaspoon rice vinegar
- Salt to taste

Method:

1. Preheat your oven 200 degrees F.
2. Spray tofu cubes with oil.
3. Add to the air fryer.
4. Cook at 375 degrees F for 15 minutes, turning once or twice.
5. In a bowl, mix the remaining ingredients.
6. Transfer to a pan over medium heat.
7. Bring to a boil.
8. Reduce heat and simmer until thickened.
9. Toss tofu in sauce before serving.

Serving Suggestions: Garnish with sesame seeds.

Preparation & Cooking Tips: Dry tofu with paper towels before cooking.

Roasted Potatoes

Preparation Time: 10 minutes

Cooking Time: 25 minutes

Servings: 4

Ingredients:

- 1 ½ lb. potatoes, diced
- Cooking spray
- Salt and pepper to taste
- ½ teaspoon garlic powder
- ½ teaspoon dried oregano
- ½ teaspoon dried basil

Method:

1. Spray potatoes with oil.
2. Season with salt, herb and spices.
3. Air fry at 400 degrees F for 20 to 25 minutes, flipping once or twice.

Serving Suggestions: Serve with mayo or ranch dip.

Preparation & Cooking Tips: Cook for 5 more minutes if you want potatoes crispier.

Cauliflower with Parmesan Cheese

Preparation Time: 10 minutes

Cooking Time: 15 minutes

Servings: 4

Ingredients:

- 3 cups cauliflower florets
- 3 teaspoons vegetable oil, divided
- 1 clove garlic, minced
- ½ teaspoon dried thyme, crushed
- ¼ cup Parmesan cheese, shredded
- ¼ cup breadcrumbs
- ¼ cup almonds, chopped

Method:

1. Toss cauliflower florets in 2 teaspoons oil and garlic.
2. Place in the Innsky Air Fryer Oven.
3. Cook at 360 degrees F for 10 minutes, stirring once.
4. Toss in remaining oil and stir in the remaining ingredients.
5. Cook in the air fryer for another 5 minutes.

Serving Suggestions: Serve with meat main courses or grilled dishes.

Preparation & Cooking Tips: You can replace chopped almonds with chopped walnuts.

Balsamic Carrots

Preparation Time: 10 minutes

Cooking Time: 10 minutes

Servings: 4

Ingredients:

- 1 tablespoon olive oil
- Salt and pepper to taste
- 1 teaspoon honey
- 1 lb. baby carrots
- 1 tablespoon melted butter
- 1 tablespoon balsamic glaze

Method:

1. Combine oil, salt, pepper and honey in a bowl.
2. Stir in carrots.
3. Coat evenly with mixture.
4. Air fry at 390 degrees F for 10 minutes, stirring once.
5. Drizzle with butter and balsamic glaze.

Serving Suggestions: Sprinkle with chopped chives.

Preparation & Cooking Tips: You can also use regular carrots. Simply slice before cooking.

Roasted Okra

Preparation Time: 5 minutes

Cooking Time: 15 minutes

Serving: 1

Ingredients:

- ½ lb. okra, trimmed and sliced
- 1 teaspoon olive oil
- Salt and pepper to taste

Method:

1. Preheat your air fryer to 350 degrees F.
2. Drizzle okra with olive oil.
3. Sprinkle with salt and pepper.
4. Transfer to the air fryer.
5. Cook for 15 minutes, stirring every 5 minutes.

Serving Suggestions: Adjust seasoning before serving.

Preparation & Cooking Tips: You can also season with garlic powder.

Onions & Sweet Peppers

Preparation Time: 15 minutes

Cooking Time: 10 minutes

Servings: 4

Ingredients:

- 1 white onion, sliced
- 3 red bell peppers, sliced
- 2 green bell peppers, sliced
- 1 tablespoon olive oil
- Salt to taste
- 1 tablespoon fresh lime juice

Method:

1. Preheat your air fryer to 350 degrees F.
2. Toss onions and peppers in oil and salt.
3. Air fry for 10 minutes, stirring once.
4. Drizzle with lime juice.

Serving Suggestions: Garnish with fresh cilantro.

Preparation & Cooking Tips: Use freshly squeezed lime juice.

Savory Mushrooms

Preparation Time: 10 minutes

Cooking Time: 10 minutes

Servings: 2

Ingredients:

- 2 tablespoons avocado oil
- 8 oz. mushrooms, sliced
- ½ teaspoon garlic powder
- 1 teaspoon soy sauce
- Salt and pepper to taste

Method:

1. Preheat your air fryer to 375 degrees F.
2. Combine all the ingredients in a bowl.
3. Transfer to the Innsky Air Fryer Oven.
4. Air fry for 10 minutes, stirring once.

Serving Suggestions: Garnish with chopped parsley.

Preparation & Cooking Tips: Use cremini or button mushrooms for this recipe.

Chapter 10: Dessert Recipes

Churros with Chocolate

Preparation Time: 45 minutes

Cooking Time: 30 minutes

Servings: 12

Ingredients:

- ¼ cup butter
- ¼ teaspoon salt
- ½ cup water
- ½ cup all purpose flour
- 2 eggs, beaten
- 2 teaspoons ground cinnamon
- ¼ cup sugar
- 2 tablespoons butter
- 4 oz. baking chocolate, chopped
- 3 tablespoons heavy cream
- 2 tablespoons vanilla kefir

Method:

1. Add butter, salt and water to a pan over medium heat.
2. Bring to a boil.
3. Reduce heat and simmer while adding flour and stirring.
4. Cook for 30 seconds.
5. Stir and cook for another 2 minutes.
6. Transfer to a bowl.

7. Add eggs to the mixture.

8. Transfer this to a piping bag with a star tip.

9. Refrigerate for 30 minutes.

10. Pipe the mixture into the air fryer.

11. Air fry at 380 degrees F for 10 minutes.

12. In a bowl, combine cinnamon and sugar.

13. Brush churros with butter.

14. Roll with cinnamon mixture.

15. Mix the remaining ingredients in a pan over medium heat.

16. Cook for 1 minute, stirring frequently.

17. Serve churros with chocolate.

Serving Suggestions: Sprinkle with additional cinnamon powder.

Strawberry Pop Tarts

Preparation Time: 25 minutes

Cooking Time: 1 hour

Servings: 6

Ingredients:

- ¼ cup granulated sugar
- 8 oz. strawberries
- ½ pie crust
- Cooking spray
- 1 tablespoon candy sprinkles

Method:

1. Mix sugar and strawberries in a bowl.
2. Microwave on high for 10 minutes.
3. Stir and microwave for another 10 minutes.
4. Let cool for 30 minutes.
5. Roll out the crust on a surface dusted with flour.
6. Slice into rectangles.
7. Top strawberry mixture.
8. Top with another rectangle sheet.
9. Seal the edges by pressing with a fork.
10. Spray with oil.
11. Cook in the air fryer at 350 degrees F for 10 minutes.

Serving Suggestions: Dust with powdered sugar.

Preparation & Cooking Tips: Freeze and reheat for later serving.

Peach Pies

Preparation Time: 30 minutes
Cooking Time: 15 minutes
Servings: 8

Ingredients:

- 2 peaches, chopped
- 1 teaspoon vanilla extract
- 3 tablespoons sugar
- 1 tablespoon lemon juice
- Salt to taste
- 1 teaspoon cornstarch
- 14 oz. pie crusts
- Cooking spray

Method:

1. In a bowl, mix peaches, vanilla extract, sugar, lemon juice and salt.
2. Let sit for 15 minutes.
3. Drain mixture. Reserve 1 tablespoon of liquid in a bowl.
4. Add cornstarch into the reserved mixture.
5. Return to the peaches.
6. Cut circles from the pie crusts.
7. Top with filling.
8. Fold and seal edges by pressing with a fork.
9. Spray with oil.
10. Air fry at 350 degrees F for 15 minutes.

Serving Suggestions: Drizzle with honey or maple syrup.

Preparation & Cooking Tips: Freeze and reheat for later serving.

Cinnamon Apple Chips

Preparation Time: 10 minutes

Cooking Time: 25 minutes

Servings: 4

Ingredients:

- 1 apple, sliced thinly
- 2 teaspoons oil
- 1 teaspoon ground cinnamon
- 1 teaspoon honey
- 1 tablespoon almond butter
- ¼ cup Greek yogurt

Method:

1. Toss apple slices in oil.
2. Sprinkle with cinnamon.
3. Air fry apple slices at 375 degrees F for 12 minutes, flipping every 4 minutes.
4. Combine remaining ingredients.
5. Serve apple chips with dip.

Serving Suggestions: Drizzle with honey.

Preparation & Cooking Tips: Use low-fat yogurt.

Cookies

Preparation Time: 5 minutes

Cooking Time: 12 minutes

Servings: 1

Ingredients:

- 2 oz. refrigerated cookie dough

Method:

1. Preheat your air fryer to 350 degrees F.
2. Air fry refrigerated cookies for 8 minutes.
3. Flip and cook for another 4 minutes.

Serving Suggestions: Serve with milk.

Preparation & Cooking Tips: Double the recipe to make more cookies.

Chapter 11: 30-Day Meal Plan

Week 1

Sunday

Breakfast: Baked egg cups

Lunch: Lemon pepper shrimp

Dinner: Beef tenderloin

Monday

Breakfast: Ham & veggie omelette

Lunch: Mongolian beef

Dinner: Fish sticks

Tuesday

Breakfast: Breakfast frittata

Lunch: Tuna patties

Dinner: Sweet & sour pork

Wednesday

Breakfast: Breakfast sausage

Lunch: Korean pork

Dinner: Rib eye steak

Thursday

Breakfast: Breakfast bombs

Lunch: Cajun shrimp

Dinner: Steak & veggies

Friday

Breakfast: Breakfast egg rolls

Lunch: Pork belly bites

Dinner: Roast beef

Saturday

Breakfast: Baked egg cups

Lunch: Sesame chicken

Dinner: Lobster tails

Week 2

Sunday

Breakfast: Ham & veggie omelette

Lunch: Lemon pepper shrimp

Dinner: Rib eye steak

Monday

Breakfast: Breakfast potatoes

Lunch: Buttermilk fried chicken

Dinner: Garlic parmesan salmon

Tuesday

Breakfast: Breakfast sausage

Lunch: Fish sticks

Dinner: Blackened chicken

Wednesday

Breakfast: Breakfast bombs

Lunch: Shrimp with spicy remoulade sauce

Dinner: Spiced pork tenderloin

Thursday

Breakfast: French toast

Lunch: Meatloaf

Dinner: Steak & mushrooms

Friday

Breakfast: Breakfast pockets

Lunch: Lemon garlic salmon

Dinner: Chicken tenderloin

Saturday

Breakfast: Breakfast casserole

Lunch: Lobster tails

Dinner: Korean pork

Week 3

Sunday

Breakfast: Breakfast egg rolls

Lunch: Pork chops & broccoli

Dinner: Buttermilk fried chicken

Monday

Breakfast: Breakfast sausage

Lunch: Meatloaf

Dinner: Crispy chicken thighs

Tuesday

Breakfast: Baked egg cups

Lunch: Tuna patties

Dinner: Pork belly bites

Wednesday

Breakfast: French toast

Lunch: Maple chicken

Dinner: Beef tips

Thursday

Breakfast: Breakfast frittata

Lunch: Fried chicken

Dinner: Shrimp with spicy remoulade sauce

Friday

Breakfast: Breakfast casserole

Lunch: Mustard pork

Dinner: Lemon garlic salmon

Saturday

Breakfast: Breakfast pockets

Lunch: Cajun shrimp

Dinner: Roast beef

Week 4

Sunday

Breakfast: Breakfast potatoes

Lunch: Crispy chicken thighs

Dinner: Garlic parmesan salmon

Monday

Breakfast: French toast

Lunch: Sweet & sour pork

Dinner: Blackened chicken

Tuesday

Breakfast: Breakfast pockets

Lunch: Beef tips

Dinner: Chicken breast

Wednesday

Breakfast: Breakfast bombs

Lunch: Pork chops & broccoli

Dinner: Steak & veggies

Thursday

Breakfast: Breakfast frittata

Lunch: Fried chicken

Dinner: Breaded pork chops

Friday

Breakfast: Breakfast potatoes

Lunch: Spiced pork tenderloin

Dinner: Mongolian beef

Saturday

Breakfast: Ham & veggie omelette

Lunch: Pork chops

Dinner: Maple chicken

Conclusion

Getting an air fryer is a great choice for anyone who wants to start eating healthily. Air fryers can cook with around 80 percent less oil making them better options than most conventional appliances.

One great advantage of air fryers than bulky ovens is their power and size. Imagine craving for crispy French fries, and you have to heat up an entire oven for a bowl of snack. With an air fryer, you get to use less energy and cook more quickly, saving you money down the line.

Innsky air fryers are made from food-grade stainless steel and BPA-free plastic to guarantee your safety. You'll be getting your money's worth since it is manufactured from durable materials that will definitely last. The product comes with a minimum of 18 months of warranty and lifetime customer support.

You can create breakfast, lunch, dinner, snacks, and desserts with a single cooker by using your Innsky air fryer. It's a good appliance to get for young families and those with limited spaces in their kitchen.

Beginner cooks will surely love the built-in presets and free recipe book. Get one for yourself and gift some to your loved ones and try exciting and mouth-watering recipes for everyone to enjoy.

Lightning Source UK Ltd.
Milton Keynes UK
UKHW020739301121
394820UK00006B/581